RECYCLE IT!

by
Mary Boone

PEBBLE
a capstone imprint

Pebble Explore is published by Pebble, an imprint of Capstone.
1710 Roe Crest Drive, North Mankato, Minnesota 56003
www.capstonepub.com

Library of Congress Cataloging-in-Publication Data is available on the Library of Congress website.
ISBN 978-1-9771-2579-8 (library binding)
ISBN 978-1-9771-2593-4 (paperback)
ISBN 978-1-9771-2599-6 (ebook pdf)

Summary: Introduces early readers to environmentalist concepts including recycling and composting, and what they can do to help the environment.

Editorial Credits
Emily Raij, editor; Brann Garvey, designer; Svetlana Zhurkin, media researcher; Katy LaVigne, production specialist

Image Credits
iStockphoto: FangXiaNuo, 16, kirin_photo, 29; Newscom: Cover Images/ Clean the World, 25; Shutterstock: Africa Studio, 13, Arunee H, 21, Fedor Korolevskiy, 11, Olha1981, 9, Phovoir, 20, Pixavril, 23, Rawpixel, cover, 17, Rich Carey, 8, Rob Crandall, 15, Roman Mikhailiuk, 7, sirtravelalot, 10, TinnaPong, 5, wavebreakmedia, 19, yoshi0511, 27

All internet sites appearing in back matter were available and accurate when this book was sent to press.

Printed and bound in the USA.
PA117

TABLE OF CONTENTS

Words in **bold** are in the glossary.

SO MUCH GARBAGE!

Look in your garbage can. Hold your nose! But really look. What's in there? Probably a lot of stuff! The average person in the United States makes 1,642 pounds (745 kilograms) per year! We are running out of places to put that garbage.

Much of that trash doesn't need to end up in the **landfill**. There are many things we can use again. Or we can use less. We can also recycle. Recycling makes trash into new things. That helps our planet.

In the U.S., more than 265 million tons of garbage is thrown out each year. A lot of that garbage is put into dumps and landfills.

As the trash breaks down, it gives off harmful **chemicals**. They enter the soil. They flow into our water. Gases go into our air. This causes **pollution**. Our water and air become unsafe. But we need them to stay clean. That keeps us healthy.

Trash also hurts our oceans. Eight million tons of garbage ends up in the oceans each year. Some is **litter**. Some travels through streams. And the wind blows some there.

There are five main spots where trash gathers in the oceans. The Great Pacific Garbage Patch is the biggest. It has 1.8 trillion pieces of plastic. It weighs about the same as 500 jumbo jets! All that trash makes animals, fish, and plants sick. It can make people sick too if they eat sick fish.

OCEAN GARBAGE PATCHES

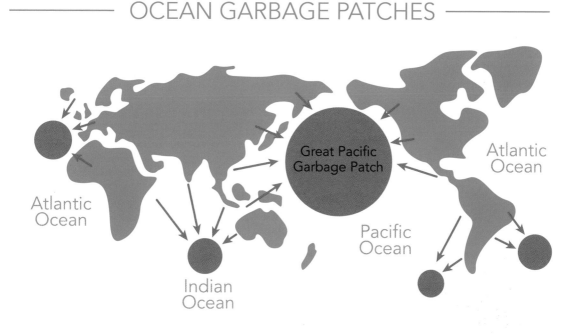

WHY RECYCLING MATTERS

Recycling helps the **environment**. Fewer new materials are needed to make things. Old paper can be recycled into new paper. Then fewer forests need to be cut down.

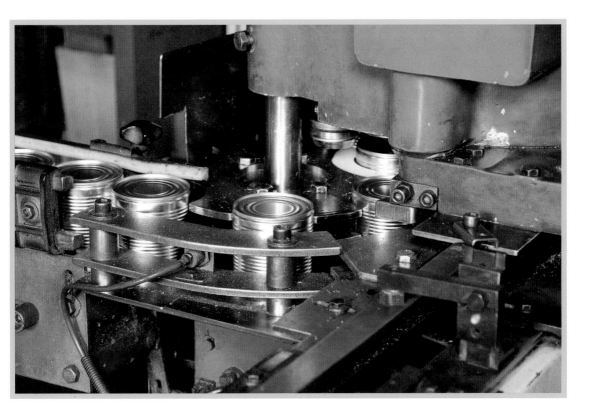

There's another plus. It takes less **energy** to make things from recycled materials than from new ones. Making new cans from recycled ones takes 95 percent less energy.

Recycled goods come in all shapes and sizes. Sometimes recycled cans are made into new cans. Other times, recycled things look nothing like what they started out as.

Recycled plastic bottles can be made into football jerseys. Carpet can be used to make notebook covers. Airbags from old cars can become backpacks. Benches can be made from recycled juice pouches.

RECYCLING AT HOME

Recycling is one of the easiest ways you can help Earth. There are **programs** all over the United States. Some cities pick up recycling from your house. You just put it in bins. These are separate from your trash. In other places, you take items to centers.

Seven of every 10 items you throw away can be recycled! Some common examples are soda cans and plastic water bottles. You can recycle cardboard boxes and glass jars too.

Does your family recycle at home? If not, it's easy to start. If you do, can you recycle even more?

Paper scraps can be recycled. So can clean cardboard food boxes. Glass jars and aluminum cans go in the bin too. Don't forget plastic bottles. There are also centers that take clothing, batteries, and electronics.

RECYCLING AT SCHOOL

Schools make a lot of trash. Many of them have recycling programs. Does your school? If not, can one be started? If there is a program, can you make it better?

Start by looking at your school's trash. What is thrown away most? What can be recycled? Is there a lot of paper in there? Ask if a paper recycling program can be started. Broken crayons can be sent to a recycling program.

People may not recycle if they don't know how. Signs can help. They show which bins to put papers or plastic in. Maybe your school needs more signs. Then students can sort before the bins get picked up.

Orange County Public Schools in Florida has a successful program. They recycle 100 million pounds each year. They recycle everything from notebook paper to cell phones.

FROM GARBAGE TO GIFTS

Food makes up one-fourth of what we throw away. But you can **compost** food instead. Composting is like recycling. It turns food scraps into something new.

Composting breaks down natural materials. That can be things like fruit peels and eggshells. Over time, these turn into a dark mix. It looks like dirt. This is compost. It is a good **fertilizer**. It helps plants grow. Composting keeps food out of landfills. It becomes something useful.

Did you know soap can be recycled? Some hotels recycle soap that guests have used. The hotels send the soap to Clean the World. This group melts the soap down. The soap is made into new bars. The bars are sent to countries all over the world.

You can help Clean the World. Kids and adults can sort the soaps. They also sort bottles of bodywash and shampoo. Sorting happens in Orlando, Las Vegas, and Hong Kong.

Kids sorting soap and bottles for Clean the World

MGM Resorts found a way to recycle oyster shells. People eat oysters at restaurants. The shells are left over. MGM Resorts workers wash the shells. They send the shells to oyster **habitats**. Each half shell becomes a home for about 10 baby oysters. More than 16 million baby oysters have grown so far!

These shells make a healthier ocean. The program keeps about 20,000 pounds (9,072 kg) of shells out of landfills each year.

As more trash is made, landfills grow. It's a problem. We can't count on other people to solve it. Everyone must help.

Start by recycling what you use. Sort aluminum, plastic, paper, and glass. Keep those out of your garbage. This cuts down on pollution. And it's an easy way to help the planet.

GLOSSARY

chemical (KEH-muh-kuhl)—a substance used in or produced through chemistry

compost (KOM-pohst)—to change decaying leaves, vegetables, and other items into a mix that makes soil better for gardening

energy (EH-nuhr-jee)—usable power that comes from sources such as electricity or heat

environment (in-VY-ruhn-muhnt)—all of the trees, plants, water, and dirt

fertilizer (FUHR-tuh-ly-zuhr)—a substance used to make plants grow better

habitat (HAB-uh-tat)—the natural place and conditions in which a plant or animal lives

landfill (LAND-fil)—a place where garbage is buried

litter (LIT-ur)—trash thrown about or in public places

pollution (puh-LOO-shuhn)—materials that hurt Earth's water, air, and land

program (PROH-gram)—a plan of actions done to reach a specific goal or result

READ MORE

French, Jess. *What a Waste: Trash, Recycling, and Protecting Our Planet.* New York: DK Publishing, 2019.

Jimenez, Vita. *Reduce, Reuse, Recycle!: Caring for Our Planet.* Minneapolis: Cantata Learning, 2017.

Lord, Michelle. *The Mess That We Made.* New York: Flashlight Press, 2020.

INTERNET SITES

Environmental Education for Kids
eekwi.org/earth/recycle/index.htm

The Greens
www.meetthegreens.org/

Keep America Beautiful
berecycled.org/

INDEX